DOLPHINS

SEYMOUR SIMON

An Imprint of HarperCollins*Publishers*

In loving memory of Joyce

Special thanks to Don E. Wilson, Senior Scientist, National Museum of Natural History, Smithsonian Institution, for his invaluable contribution to this book.

PHOTO CREDITS: page 4: © Stephen Frink/Getty Images; pages 7, 10, 23, 24: © SeaPics.com; page 8: © DiMaggio/Kalish/CORBIS; page 11: © Brandon Cole/Visuals Unlimited; page 12: © altrendo nature/Getty Images; page 15: © Rod Haestier/Getty Images; page 16: Francois Gohier/Photo Researchers, Inc; page 17: © Gerard Lacz/Animals Animals Enterprises; page 19: © Albert Gea/Reuters/CORBIS; page 20: © Paul Katz/Getty Images; page 25: Gregory Ochocki/Photo Researchers, Inc.; page 27: © Tom Brakefield/CORBIS; page 28: © Fred Whitehead/Animals Animals Enterprises; page 31: © Andy Rouse/Jupiter Images

Collins is an imprint of HarperCollins Publishers.

Dolphins

Manufactured in China.

For information address HarperCollins Children's Books, a division of HarperCollins Publishers, 1350 Avenue of the Americas, New York, NY 10019.
www.harpercollinschildrens.com

Library of Congress Cataloging-in-Publication Data

Simon, Seymour.
Dolphins / Seymour Simon. — 1st ed.
p. cm.
ISBN 978-0-06-028393-3 (trade bdg.) — ISBN 978-0-06-028394-0 (lib bdg.)
1. Dolphins—Juvenile literature. I. Title.
QL737.C432S547 2009 2008010654
599.53—dc22 CIP
AC

---

1 2 3 4 5 6 7 8 9 10
❖
First Edition

Smithsonian Mission Statement

For more than 160 years, the Smithsonian has remained true to its mission, "the increase and diffusion of knowledge." Today the Smithsonian is not only the world's largest provider of museum experiences supported by authoritative scholarship in science, history, and the arts but also an international leader in scientific research and exploration. The Smithsonian offers the world a picture of America, and America a picture of the world.

In a world where so many wild animals avoid and fear humans, dolphins charm us because they often seem unafraid of people. Clever, curious, and mischievous, dolphins love to play and have fun.

A dolphin nicknamed Simo lived in the waters off Solva, South Wales. Simo seemed to enjoy capsizing canoes and overturning the people in them. He would follow a diver underwater, suddenly appear from behind, and rise up to hit him on the head, knocking off his snorkel and goggles.

One bottlenose dolphin nicknamed Percy, who lived in the coastal waters near Cornwall, England, played with the crab pots that people placed on the sea bottom. He seemed to delight in lifting boat anchors and moving the boats to different spots.

There are countless stories of dolphins befriending people and even helping them to survive at sea. Sailors believed that dolphins brought them luck and that it was a bad omen to kill a dolphin. In the past, fisherfolk would set dolphins free if they got entangled in their nets.

Dolphins and porpoises are whales, or cetaceans (the scientific name for whales). Dolphins and porpoises are smaller, toothed whales. Larger whales such as the blue whale have a comblike strainer made of baleen, or whalebone, in their mouths instead of teeth. Blue whales are the largest animals on Earth, growing to more than 100 feet in length and weighing over 150 tons. Most dolphins and porpoises are smaller than 12 feet long.

Names can be confusing. Some porpoises are called dolphins, some dolphins are called porpoises, and a few dolphins are called whales. The largest dolphin is the orca, or killer whale. A male orca can grow to 30 feet in length, much bigger than other dolphins but much smaller than baleen whales.

All whales are mammals. That means that they are warm-blooded, have babies that are born alive and feed on milk, and have hair or fur on some part of their bodies. Whales live in water but have lungs. When they come to the surface, they breathe air through an opening on top of their heads called a blowhole. When a whale surfaces, it spouts a "blow" of water vapor.

What's the difference between a dolphin and a porpoise? Not that much. Dolphins and porpoises look and act very much alike. Both have streamlined bodies, tail flukes, and blowholes. Porpoises are usually smaller and rarely longer than seven feet in length. Most dolphins are not longer than ten feet.

Perhaps the best way to tell dolphins and porpoises apart is by their heads and bodies. Porpoises have smaller heads and lack a beak or snout. The top, or dorsal, fin on a porpoise is triangular like the dorsal fin of a shark. The dorsal fin of a dolphin is rounded like a wave. A porpoise's teeth are spade shaped, while a dolphin's teeth are cone shaped. Dolphins have lean, streamlined bodies. Porpoises often look chubby or chunky by comparison.

Porpoises are rarely seen on the surface of the water. Dolphins often swim on or just below the surface, riding the bow waves of fishing boats. Dolphins also show less fear of humans than porpoises do.

There are about thirty-five different species, or kinds, of dolphins and six kinds of porpoises. Most of these live in the salty oceans, but four dolphin species live in freshwater rivers. Five or six kinds of dolphins, including the orca and pilot whale, are usually called whales.

Freshwater river dolphins live in only a few of the largest rivers of Asia and South America, such as the Ganges, the Indus, and the Amazon Rivers. Dolphins and porpoises live in all of the oceans except for the very coldest polar waters.

The common dolphin, the Atlantic spotted and the Atlantic striped dolphins, and the white-beaked and the bottlenose dolphins are often seen in the North Atlantic Ocean. Pacific white-sided and bottlenose dolphins live in waters off Canada and Alaska. Spinner dolphins, Risso's dolphins, and rough-toothed dolphins are mostly found in warmer tropical waters.

Dolphins live and feed in large family groups where warm and cold currents meet and the waters are rich in food and nutrients. Dolphins may travel hundreds of miles in search of a variety of fish, squid, and shrimp.

Despite their sharp teeth, dolphins don't chew their food. They use their teeth for grabbing and holding prey. Dolphins usually swallow fish whole.

Some dolphins feed at night, while others feed during the day. A group of bottlenose dolphins, called a pod, often works together to catch fish. In open waters, the dolphins encircle a school of fish and herd them into a small area. Then the dolphins take turns charging through the midst of the school to feed. Dolphins sometimes use their tail flukes to bat larger fish into the air, stunning them so they're easier to catch. Other times, dolphins herd schools of fish toward shore to trap them in shallow water where they can't get away.

Dolphins and porpoises use different sounds to communicate with each other. The sounds include whistles, clicks, barks, squawks, and rasps. To signal others in their pod they also jump straight out of the water and fall back with a loud splash. Some people think that dolphin sounds are a form of language.

Dolphins can produce a series of 2,000 high-pitched clicks per second that go through the water, hit an object, and bounce back to the sender. By listening to the echo and the time it took to return, a dolphin can accurately locate a fish as small as your little finger. This is called echolocation, or sonar.

Dolphins scan objects with their sonar. They can also combine the sonar image with their vision so that they can identify objects. Dolphins use their sonar to find food or swim at night when there is no light to see their surroundings.

Dolphins and porpoises are social animals that live in groups of all sizes. Small groups are called pods. The size of a pod depends upon the kind of dolphin, the age and sex, and other conditions. Pods range in size from two or three to a dozen or more. Several pods sometimes join into herds or schools and can number in the hundreds.

Dolphins in a pod have strong bonds. They can even recognize each other after a long separation. Mother-calf bonds are long lasting. A calf stays with its mother for three or more years.

Young adult male pods are strong and long lasting. The young males cooperate in hunting and survival. Dolphins establish dominance in a pod by biting, chasing, and smacking their tails on the water. They scratch each other with their teeth and leave tooth marks. Dolphins also use bubble clouds from their blowholes to show their place of power in the pod.

Dolphin mothers give birth to a single calf just below the surface of the water. The baby dolphin nurses underwater from its mother but has to come to the surface to breathe. At birth, a baby dolphin weighs thirty to fifty pounds and is thirty-five to fifty inches long.

A calf will nurse for about a year and a half. Babies are toothless at birth but start to grow teeth in a few weeks. When it is about four months old, a baby starts to eat fish but continues to nurse as well.

Dolphin mothers are very protective of their babies. A young dolphin can easily stray from the pod and get lost or attacked by sharks if it is not constantly watched. A mother often raises her calf with the help of other female dolphins in the pod called aunties. When the mother is resting, the aunties act as babysitters, swimming around the calf in protective circles. The close contact between the calf and other dolphins helps the youngster learn how to fish and swim and communicate with and live with others in the pod.

The bottlenose dolphin may be the best known because it is often seen in marine parks and other large aquariums. The bottlenose is seen along the shores of the United States and lives in temperate and tropical waters around the world.

This dolphin gets its name because of its short and stubby beak that resembles a bottle. Its top fin is high and curved and located near the middle of its back. Its flippers are medium length and pointed. Male bottlenoses are usually larger than females and may reach 12 feet in length and weigh 1,400 pounds. Their color is usually light gray to slate gray on the upper parts of the body, becoming lighter on the sides and pink gray on the bottom.

Bottlenoses live in groups of twenty or less near the shore but may live in offshore groups of several hundred. An adult bottlenose eats fifteen to thirty pounds of food each day. At times, bottlenoses feed near fishing boats.

Swimming at speeds of over thirty miles per hour and often riding the bow waves of boats, Dall's porpoise is the fastest-moving dolphin or porpoise. The head and the back of the porpoise create a hollow cone of air that allows the Dall to breathe while still riding the underwater wave. Dalls live only in the North Pacific, from Baja California to Alaska and across the Bering Sea into Japanese waters.

The beautifully marked black-and-white porpoise was named after American naturalist W. H. Dall. A Dall's small, round head appears even smaller than it is because of the porpoise's strong, muscular body. A Dall is quite small compared to other dolphins, averaging 6 feet and weighing between 250 and 300 pounds.

A Dall's teeth are unusual. Each tooth is separated by rigid growths called gum-teeth. Because the regular teeth are so small, these horny growths help in grasping slippery foods. A Dall's eyes are also exceptionally colored, with deep, shiny blue-green pupils.

The Amazon River dolphin, or boto, is one of the few dolphins that live in freshwater. Botos live throughout the Amazon and the Orinoco river basins in South America. Amazon River peoples rarely hunted river dolphins. They feared that harming a boto would cause their children to be born with a disease in which the skull remains open like the blowhole of the dolphin.

A boto is born with dark gray skin. As the boto grows older, its skin begins to turn bright pink. Botos have long beaks with many stiff hairs. Scientists think that the botos' hairs are used as feelers to help them navigate in the muddy river waters.

Botos, like most dolphins, can change the shape of their melons, an organ in their heads that scientists believe provides a means of focusing the sounds used in echolocation. They can also scan—turn their heads from side to side, focusing in the direction of the sound waves.

Orcas (killer whales) are the largest dolphins in the world. An orca's back and sides are jet black and it has a gleaming white underbelly and a white oval spot above each eye. The coloring of an orca may remind you of a penguin. A male orca can grow to be thirty-two feet long, as large as a school bus, and weigh eight to nine tons, as much as three Asian elephants. Orcas live in all the oceans of the world.

Orcas care for sick and injured members of their pod. Each orca pod makes some sounds in common with other pods and other sounds that only are made by their own pod.

Orcas live and hunt in pods of several females, calves, juveniles, and one or more males. Sometimes they are called the wolves of the seas. Depending upon the area, orcas feed on different kinds of food, including sea lions, elephant seals, harbor seals, smaller porpoises, penguins, small as well as larger whales, and fish including sharks. Orcas do not attack people in the wild.

The greatest threats to dolphins and porpoises are still pollution and careless commercial net fishing. Scientists think that increased levels of garbage and industrial wastes washing into the sea help create a red tide. A red tide is the result of the rapid growth of tiny sea plankton that produce a kind of poison. Fish eat the poison, and dolphins eat the fish and die. During a red tide, many dolphins may be killed or injured.

In the Pacific Ocean, tuna swim with dolphins. More than fifty years ago, many thousands of dolphins were killed in tuna nets every year. Today different kinds of tuna nets and careful fishing boat captains have reduced the number of dolphins killed to a few thousand. And divers and sailors release any dolphins caught in the nets.

People are the greatest threat to dolphins, but people can also help dolphins the most. If people buy tuna that is labeled "dolphin safe" on the can, then commercial tuna fishermen will use safety nets that don't accidentally ensnare dolphins. The United States Congress passed the Marine Mammal Protection Act to protect whales, dolphins, and porpoises.

Here are some things we can all do to help dolphins:

• Put beach litter into a trash container.

• If you are in a boat when you spot dolphins, ask the driver to slow down and avoid turning or reversing suddenly. Do not harass dolphins, and don't pursue them if they leave.

• Help beached dolphins and porpoises by calling the local police, aquarium, or department of conservation.

• Write letters to government officials asking them to strengthen the protection of animals.

GLOSSARY

Baleen—Also called whalebone and made of the same substance as human hair, only much thicker and stronger, almost like a broom. Some whales have two thick rows of baleen instead of teeth.

Calf—A baby dolphin or porpoise.

Cetaceans—Mammals, including whales, dolphins, and porpoises, that have adapted to life in the water.

Dorsal fin—A fin on the backs of some fish, whales, dolphins, and porpoises that keeps them from rolling in the water and helps them make sudden turns while swimming. Dorsal fins are unique, like human fingerprints.

Flippers—Flat limbs used for swimming and steering.

Marine Mammal Protection Act—A law passed on October 21, 1972, making it against the law to harass, hunt, capture, or kill mammals that live in the water.

Melon—A large, fatty organ in a whale, dolphin, or porpoise's brain that helps them measure the return of their sound signals when they use echolocation, or sonar.

Pod—A social group of whales, dolphins, or porpoises.

River basin—An area of land where smaller streams and rivers come together to make one big river that flows into an ocean.

Tail flukes—The flat, wide tail fins of whales, dolphins, and porpoises.

INDEX

READ MORE ABOUT IT

Smithsonian Institution
www.si.edu

The Dolphin Institute
www.dolphin-institute.org

OCEANS
by Seymour Simon

PENGUINS
by Seymour Simon

SHARKS
by Seymour Simon

WHALES
by Seymour Simon